MW00365061

Mother's
daze

To my wonderful
friend Helen who
has bailed me out of
many gardening
dilemas

Love [signature]

Mother's daze

JANE ISFELD STILL

CFI
SPRINGVILLE, UT

© 2010 Jane Isfeld Still

All rights reserved.

No part of this book may be reproduced in any form whatsoever, whether by graphic, visual, electronic, film, microfilm, tape recording, or any other means, without prior written permission of the publisher, except in the case of brief passages embodied in critical reviews and articles.

This is not an official publication of The Church of Jesus Christ of Latter-day Saints. The opinions and views expressed herein belong solely to the author and do not necessarily represent the opinions or views of Cedar Fort, Inc. Permission for the use of sources, graphics, and photos is also solely the responsibility of the author.

ISBN 13: 978-1-59955-387-0

Published by CFI, an imprint of Cedar Fort, Inc., 2373 W. 700 S., Springville, UT, 84663
Distributed by Cedar Fort, Inc., www.cedarfort.com

LIBRARY OF CONGRESS CATALOGING-IN-PUBLICATION DATA

Still, Jane Isfeld, 1954–
Mother's daze / Jane Isfeld Still.
    p. cm.
ISBN 978-1-59955-387-0
1. Motherhood—Humor. I. Title.

HQ759.S694 2010
306.874'3—dc22

                    2009043840

Illustrated by Matt Kelley
Cover and page design by Angela D. Olsen
Cover design © 2010 by Lyle Mortimer
Edited by Katherine Carter

Printed in Canada

10 9 8 7 6 5 4 3 2 1

Printed on acid-free paper

Dedication

I WOULD LIKE TO DEDICATE THIS BOOK
TO MY FAMILY,
WHO KEEP ME HUMBLE
AND ARE MY INSPIRATION.

Contents

CHAPTER 1
An Eye for Discipline

I SCRUTINIZED MY PROFILE IN THE MIRROR. Nothing. Not one speck of difference. My jaw ached from the stretching, grimacing, and contorting I had inflicted on it all month during my daily face aerobic routine. The only position I found that gave me the firm, sleek jawline I longed for was made by jutting out my chin. But then I looked like a chimpanzee.

I was cursed with a weak chin that made me look like a hound dog every time I looked down. What if I passed this genetic defect on to my children? When my husband was little, he had a belly button that poked out, so my mother-in-law taped a quarter over it to push it back in. It worked. Maybe, while my children were little, I could duct tape the wobbly skin under their chins to their jawbones. It would be like preventive plastic surgery.

Rick and I had been married only six weeks when we decided to have thirteen children, including two sets of twins. At least, that's what I wanted. His eyes sort of glazed over when we discussed it. When I reminded him that I had taken a child development class in college and had all the information and confidence I needed to charge into motherhood, his face changed from a pasty gray color, to red, and then back to white again. I decided that wasn't the time to worry him with the fact that the curriculum hadn't covered physical defects, such as weak chins.

Back at my mirror, I closed my eyes to picture our little angels. In my mind, they were all decked out and adorable in white, holding hands as they skipped together through rolling green meadows and laughing as we enjoyed endless picnics together as a family. The sun shone on the snowy tablecloth that was spread over the grass. Fried chicken tempted us from our red-gingham-lined picnic basket.

Next, I pictured our perfect home. There it was—the center of activity with a jukebox, pool table, and a refrigerator full of anything our beautiful sleek-jawed children desired. One blissful moment flowed into another. I sighed. Motherhood couldn't come soon enough.

Meanwhile, back in reality, my husband and I attended a church where parents would tolerate just about any behavior from their children during our worship services from leaping off the benches to swinging from the chandeliers. To practice my future mothering abilities, I appointed myself to the position of reverence police over these unruly children and began honing my skills in the finer points of discipline. It looked like my face aerobics wouldn't go to waste after all.

For restless children sitting nearby, I met first infractions with my stern sideways glance. If that didn't work, I fixed them with a three-quarter glare. On rare occasions, I found it necessary to impart a full frontal face attack, during which my eyes became piercing pinpoints of ice. It never failed to freeze mischievous children into immediate, humble compliance.

When necessary, I zeroed my vision in like a radar beam to zing my displeasure across the room. I squinched my eyes into beady slits, pursed my lips together, and then slowly opened my left eye, lifting it a little higher than the right, to burn a gaze that motivated immediate repentance from even the most rowdy child.

With a little imagination, I conquered the problem of disciplining children sitting on the pews in front of me. To do so, I took a deep audible sigh that greatly enhanced the size of my torso, expelled it quickly, and clicked my tongue. This caused miscreant children to turn around so I could then fix them with an icy stare.

Each of my reprimanding looks was followed with a half-smile and slight nod when the child settled down. I knew the importance of reproving with love. It was all so simple.

As I watched other women handling their children, I compiled a list of things I would never tolerate: My children would obey me instantly, never scream, and always say "please" and "thank you." They would sit quietly at my feet when we were visiting and not whirl around like human eggbeaters with arms, destroying everything in their paths.

It would never occur to them to whine or beg for food. They would always be well groomed, and by no means would they ever be seen in public sporting a runny nose or dirty hands and face. As far as the terrible twos everyone sighed about, I would certainly have no problem managing a two-year-old. It was just a matter of attitude and proper training.

Spanking was absolutely unnecessary. Needing to spank showed a lack of intelligence on the part of the parent. And all that fuss about teenagers! Why, I loved teenagers, and they loved me. I couldn't wait until my children were in their teens. It would be so much fun communicating together. On and on I went.... Nobody told me I was too stupid to live.

CHAPTER 2
It's Not in My Head

I WANTED TO DANCE ON THE ROOFTOPS and shout, "I'm going to have a baby!" But I was too busy developing a close and personal relationship with the toilet. It was suppertime, and I had just discovered I couldn't cook hamburger anymore. And it was not in my head.

Luckily for Rick, he wasn't one of those know-it-all husbands who thought morning sickness was a psychological disease, or I would have been forced to puke in something of his, like his shoes, and when my vomit oozed out warm between his toes, I'd sneer, "It's only your imagination."

I find it ludicrous that some men, including doctors, have the nerve to suppose that throughout the entire span of history, women were so stupid that they couldn't invent a sickness a little less repulsive. If I were going to concoct a disease, it would have something to do with eating expensive chocolate. It would not involve sticking my head inside the toilet for a preview of last night's dinner being re-served in the form of warmed-over soup.

To make matters worse, I wanted to look pregnant immediately. If I kept throwing up my food, I'd never get a big tummy. I couldn't wait to buy maternity clothes. I actually felt sorry for a friend of mine who carried her baby so far back that she was still wearing her tight jeans at seven months. It wasn't until after delivery, when my stomach *still* looked like I was seven months pregnant—only mushy instead of firm—that I was insanely jealous. My choices of outfits to wear home from the hospital were my birthday suit, a queen-sized sheet, and maternity clothes. Somehow, after nine months, they weren't so cute anymore.

However, it was fortunate that I was excited to wear maternity clothes in the beginning because I gained all my weight during the first five months. For the final sixteen to eighteen weeks, I looked like I was going to drop an elephant any second. "Aren't you ever going to have that baby?" everyone would ask.

My babies never showed up on time. My theory is that they peeked down at the earth from heaven, got a glimpse of me waddling around like a moving circus tent, and had to be pulled out of me kicking and screaming.

By the time my babies were due, I was embarrassed to be seen in public. I felt gargantuan. I was an affront to the public who were forced to look at me. I was walking up the stairs in front of my cousin one day when she blurted, "Wow, have your hips ever gotten huge." What was I supposed to say? Thank you?

That was followed by a dinner out with friends during which I got stuck between the bench and the table in the restaurant. I stretched my lips into the kind of a smile that showed my gritted teeth as I listened to every hippopotamus joke ever written. I needed different friends.

The next morning I stood with my back to the full-length mirror and gazed through a smaller looking glass held in front so I could assess the volume of material stretched across the ten acres that were masquerading as my bottom. "Honey, do you think my hips are fat?"

Rick choked and bolted from the room. I don't know how a six-foot, 180-pound man can effectively hide himself in an eight-hundred-square-foot apartment, but I didn't see him for several hours.

"I'm fat," I wailed when I found him in the last place I'd ever think to look—under a car in the garage. "I can't tie my own shoes or even see my feet, and—I'm not sure—but I think I waddle when I walk."

He crawled out from under the car, stood up, and slowly wiped the grease from his hands. Obviously, sniffing gas fumes had cleared his brain. "Honey, you look beautiful. We don't want this baby cramped into a tiny little belly. Our baby deserves the penthouse suite."

The poor man meant well, but I'd never heard a worse compliment in my life. I wasn't as big as a house; I was as big as an entire hotel. At least it was a nice hotel. I would have given him a hug, but my arms weren't long enough anymore.

CHAPTER 3
The Miracle of Birth

WHEN MY HUSBAND GETS A LITTLE SNIFFLE or a cough, he drags himself onto the couch and thrashes about in an agonized fervor that would win him an Academy Award for best deathbed performance. The veins in his neck pop out as he strains to lift his head off the pillow just enough for a gasp of air, so he can then summon me from some dark recess of the basement, where I am hiding from his moans.

The first time I heard his strangled bellow, I took the stairs six at a time, crashed into the kitchen chairs, and cracked my shins. I ended up sprawled, face down, like a straw scarecrow at his feet. "Honey, are you all right?" I managed to squeak out.

"I need the remote," he said, quavering.

"Are you kidding me?" I lay bleeding and bruised on the floor, and he didn't have the good grace to be dying. His arms were stretched out, and his fingers flailed mere millimeters from his precious controller. Any self-respecting woman in the same position would take off her shirt, tie a loop in the arm, and lasso the darn thing. At the very least, she would remove a shoe and use it as an arm extension. Under no circumstances would she render herself so humiliatingly incapacitated. That was the moment I knew: If men had to give birth, their version of the phrase, "Not tonight, dear, I have a headache," would be, "Are you *crazy?*"

A woman, on the other hand, is a study in contradictions. Who else would drag herself to the grocery store in her early months of pregnancy, spend hard-earned cash on food, make the effort to cook it, and manage to be optimistic that it was not going to end up in the river via the toilet?

After she has given birth, a woman can recount every detail of the harrowing ride to the hospital, the length of her labor to the second, and exactly how many stitches the doctor inflicted. She will share those war stories with anyone who will listen, but she won't recall the pain. The real miracle of birth is the fact that a woman will go through this process more than once. How is this possible? I have a theory.

Women were created with a delete button in the brain. The umbilical cord winds through the placenta and up through all the organs, finds the secret compartment containing the button, and attaches itself. That would also explain why it takes so long for the placenta to dislodge after childbirth. It takes time to tear away from that button and pop it into delete mode before making its journey back through the body.

Scientists have not discovered this yet because it has not occurred to them to confer with computer gurus like Bill Gates on the little matter of childbirth. It makes sense, if you think about it. The tummy swells, the ankles swell, so why couldn't there be an area in the brain that swells until the little button is pushed to release a vacuum that sucks out all memory cells involving labor pain and childbirth?

If scientists have discovered the reason for this phenomenon, they're not talking about it. Why would they want to find a cure for something that they don't want to cure? After all, this would spell the end of humanity. Or worse yet, they would have to devise a way for men to repopulate the planet. Better to leave well enough alone.

CHAPTER 4
The Three-Drink Wonder

I WAS THE SIZE OF A SMALL APARTMENT building and hadn't seen my feet for weeks. If I didn't need to have Rick tie my shoes every day, I would have forgotten I even had feet. I felt as though I would be the first woman in history to carry her baby for eternity, and I was done with platitudes.

"It will come soon enough." *Oh, yeah, in whose opinion?*

"You'll be sorry when your baby is up crying all night."

"A watched pot never boils." *Okay, so I look like a pot. Do they have to rub it in?*

I'd been waddling around in a tent for nine months, and all those childbirth horror stories held no more fear. I was sick and tired of sticking close to the toilet, and, boy, was I ready to lose the fat pants.

I'd heard about a mother who wanted to deliver her baby while her husband was home on leave. She took castor oil three times a day and *wham*, her baby came a month early. It was time for me to lay up a supply of castor oil.

The thick yellow liquid dripped into my spoon. My taste buds started salivating the way they did when I was about to lose lunch. Someone told me a banana would disguise the heavy scent and flavor, so I psyched myself up for an oily banana shake. I stuffed the banana into the blender and then added a quarter cup of castor oil and a glug of milk. I chugged it then chased it with a chunk of bread to erase the aftertaste.

My husband watched with a combination of awe and revulsion. He couldn't abide the smell or taste of a banana, and watching me slip one down with castor oil turned his face green. I chased him around the kitchen, shaking the banana skin in his direction. This was what pregnancy did to a woman's mind.

I survived three more drinks that day before I was gripped with serious stomach cramps. I crawled into the tiny room that had become my second home. Before the night was over, as I sat and flushed, I repented for every disparaging comment I had ever made about my beautiful porcelain princess.

My castor oil experiment had cleaned me out, but a bright day dawned on a new scheme. This plan would challenge any Olympic contender. I hurled my bulk up and down a full flight of stairs and then raced to the mini-trampoline where I bottomed out and injured my ankles.

My mother-in-law, who had come to help when the baby came, smiled that "Are you totally insane?" smile I'd become used to seeing and gently asked, "Dear, are you trying to shake the baby out? You know, it really will come on its own. I can't remember reading of one single incident in the history of all mankind where a baby failed to make its entrance."

Well, she would know. She probably wrote the history of mankind.

CHAPTER 5
It's a Boy!

"WE HAVE A BOY, HONEY." RICK BEAMED AT me as I began to stir out of the anesthetic stupor of my C-section. So much for my mother-in-law's sage advice. Even the doctor realized this baby wasn't coming without help.

My response should have been, "Is he healthy?" or, "Does he have your nose?" But no. The first endearing words out of my mouth—after eagerly waiting more than nine months—were, "Is he ugly?" I still say it was the drugs.

"He's beautiful," my husband said.

They stopped the gurney by the nursery window, and I pulled my eyes open. Rick was a liar. Huge bug eyes swam in a pinched face. My weak chin was sucked into a large mouth. "He's ugly," I moaned, and I promptly passed out.

It's a good thing the baby couldn't voice his opinion of me in that first glance. It might have gone something like, "That woman with the stringy hair and dopey expression is my mom? What a wreck."

Within a few days, both of us shaped up, and at least one of us looked beautiful. It wasn't me.

In the months before my son's birth, I amused myself by tormenting my family and friends with my choice of names for my poor, unsuspecting infant. After all, a name is the signature statement that carries you through life and, even more importantly, makes or breaks you when you start first grade.

I'm half Icelandic, so I wanted to name one of my boys Bjorn. But even I realized how "Still, Bjorn" would sound during roll call. Regardless of how I teased about the names of my children, I did try to consider all the angles. It wasn't until years later that I discovered one had managed to slip by me. My youngest daughter, Briana, came home from school one day, put her hands on her hips, and glared at me. "Mom, how could you have done that to me?"

I was puzzled. "What did I do?"

"My name, Mom. All the kids in class made fun of me."

"What's the matter with the name Briana?"

"Think about it, Mom. Didn't you ever think what my initials would be?"

"Briana Lee Still. B. L. S. What's the matter with that?"

"B. S., Mom, B. S."

Meanwhile, I wallowed in the power of terrorizing my family with possible names for their yet unborn posterity: "If we have a boy, we could call him Pubert Edward. 'Pubert E.' has a distinctive ring."

Before I teased my family, I teased my college roommates on this topic as well. I once convinced them I would name my first-born son Rasputin and nickname him "little Razz." They were appropriately horrified.

Once I read a book in which the heroine's name was Sawyer. I actually loved that name for a girl. I told my husband and my dad, "If it's a girl, we'll call her Sawyer." I immediately recognized the "I'm too filled with horror to speak" expression on Rick's face.

My dad's eyebrows climbed to new heights, and his voice raised five decibels. "Sawyer? Are you so ignorant that you don't know what a sawyer is? You're not going to name any granddaughter of mine after an occupation for some lumberjack. I don't care if you did read it in a book. That kind of trash should be burned."

My dad's reaction only cemented my opinion that he and Archie Bunker were brothers who had been separated at birth. I looked to Rick for support. He had none to give.

"Sorry, I'm with your dad and Uncle Archie."

We finally decided on the name Clayton Dale for a boy. We would call him Clay for short. Dale was Rick's middle name. The moment of truth arrived as I held my son in my arms. I looked down at him and murmured, "Hello, baby Clay," then I burst into tears.

Rick thought I was having a tender moment until I wailed, "We can't call him Clay. He doesn't look like dirt, and I hate the name Clayton."

To make matters worse, we couldn't leave the hospital until we had filled out the proper paperwork, which included a name for the baby. Who makes up these stupid rules? It's not like I was going to run around calling him, "Hey, you," until he went to kindergarten.

This name would mold my child. That's a lot of pressure. A parent should have time to study a baby's attributes a few years before tagging him with a name that may not suit his personality.

When we got a dog, we watched her for a week or more before we realized that every time we set her on the ground, she squirted. We called her Squirt. Why couldn't we do that for our baby? Except, babies don't do much except sleep, eat, and dirty their diapers for the first three months—activities that don't inspire the most appropriate name selection.

I decided that maybe we should adopt the practice some American Indian tribes used—naming our baby after the first thing we saw when he was born. They have beautiful names for their children like Running Deer, Moonbeam, and Flower Petal. On second thought, I realized I would have to call our baby Ugly Face, since that was the first thing I saw.

I decided that next time I would consider giving birth in a mountain meadow, where something beautiful would catch my eye. For now, I gazed—for inspiration—at the sparkling commode across the room and tried to imagine a hand-carved fountain, bubbling and gurgling like a pure mountain spring: nothing came to mind, absolutely nothing.

For days, hormones dripped from the corners of my eyes as I fretted over what we would call our nameless waif. It had to be dignified, yet endearing. I phoned Rick late every evening to discover that instead of pacing the floors, he had the nerve to be laid out cold on a cushy mattress. Did he even care that I lay prostrate on my sick bed? "How can you sleep at a time like this? Don't you realize we have to name little Anonymous?"

Finally, as my nurses ticked off the seconds to check-out, sanity settled my frenzied mind—Rick's sister came up with the perfect name.

His name would be Jason Rick.

CHAPTER 6
Postpartum

NINE POUNDS OF BABY AND A PLACENTA big enough to weigh at least three pounds had been pulled from my body five days ago. I could see no justification for the fifteen-inch gap between the button and the buttonhole of my jeans. In fact, my pants were stuck at the top of my thighs, and I had to do the penguin shuffle to get back to my bed.

The first thing I had done when I could stagger around with my IV was push it to a room behind the nurse's station to weigh myself.

"Liar," I shouted at the scale and gave it a good kick. "You oversized hunk of scrap metal." My nurse rushed over to salvage its parts. "I demand a re-weigh." I shucked my slippers, then my robe, and was about to lose my air-conditioned gown too before a cold blast of air cooled my backside and checked my insanity.

"Are you kidding me? Only four pounds?" I had the sense to put my robe back on before I let my temper loose again. Two orderlies showed up out of nowhere to "help" me back to my room.

Any minute now, Rick would be here to take me and the baby home. Not only did my jeans mock me, but the upper buttons on my shirt also looked like they were a continent apart. I felt as though I were up close and personal with a pair of Mount Everests. "That would explain the scale differentiation," I muttered, looking down. "What am I supposed to do with these things? They aren't going to fit into anything I own."

I'd always thought an extra inch or two in the bust line would be nice, but this was a complete distortion of balance. I expected to fall face forward at any moment. That was all I needed—a broken nose. The swelling would surely be good for another pound or two.

I was the victim of too much television. In TV Land, the glowing mother-to-be is wheeled into the hospital, and, after a moment or two of delicate perspiration, the nurse places a beautiful bundle into her outstretched arms. Her handsome, well-groomed husband enters at the perfect moment to bestow a kiss on her brow and flash a bouquet of flowers from behind his back. Before you know it, she's strolling out of the hospital in a perfect, size-six designer frock, and the baby is snug in the crook of Daddy's arm.

Rick didn't bring me any flowers. Just because we were on a student budget and I said I'd be mad if he spent money on flowers was no reason not to bring me some. I'd told him so last night. He could have at least sprung for a balloon or a card. He didn't even bring the baby anything. What was he thinking?

Mr. Cheapskate popped through the door just then and pulled the curtain aside. "Hi, hon. You ready? How ya feeling?"

Was the man blind? My chest was burgeoning to new proportions with the influx of sustenance. My shirt was wide open, the buttons shrinking closer to my backbone by the second, and my penguin pants were still slopped around my ankles.

"Yeah. Take a picture, and then we'll go. Of course I'm not ready. My clothes shrunk, my body is still the size of half the globe, and is it possible for these things to pop?" I gazed down at my chest.

"Honey, you look beautiful. You're just having some postpartum blues."

"Don't even tell me that. I am not now, nor will I ever, have postpartum anything. I am perfectly happy; I'm just mad at the moment. If you got up one morning and you had the body of a blowfish and none of your clothes fit, you'd be a little perturbed too. Help me pull these pants off my ankles and throw me my maternity clothes."

Rick woke Jason up so I could feed him before we left, then he began gathering my things together.

"Don't put those clothes in that bag—they belong in this one. Never mind, I'll do it myself. Finish filling out this paperwork."

Rick completed the paperwork and held Jason a moment while I started to sort through the things he'd brought.

"This is not the outfit I asked you to bring for the baby, hon. I distinctly said the blue one. I told you exactly where it was."

Rick stood up. "I'm going to take these forms to the nurse and get you checked out."

"Did you listen to anything I said last night?" I called after him. "I did not want this crocheted blanket. It isn't warm enough. And these are not the right shoes."

I continued to mutter. "I can't believe he couldn't get even one thing right. I was explicit. And he has the nerve to say I'm having postpartum blues. I never heard anything so ridiculous in my life. Anyone would be frustrated in my situation. If you get frustrated before you have a baby, nobody says you have pre-partum blues." I finished spreading the baby blankets on the bed, laid Jason inside, and continued to fume.

"Men! They have a pat little label for everything. When a woman's upset over anything, no matter how valid, it must be PMS. If a man forgets their anniversary, after forgetting her birthday and Mother's Day, what does he say when you casually remind him of these infractions? 'Is it that time of the month again, dear?'

"Men use that excuse to absolve themselves from any responsibility for their actions. I think they should pay attention to their own hormones and leave ours alone. As a matter of fact, it was his hormones that got me into this mess."

I glanced toward Jason, who was sound asleep and innocent. What was I thinking? I was thrilled to be a mom. I had a perfect little boy and a wonderful husband. It wasn't Rick's fault that I had taken the term "eating for two" very literally the past nine months. As a matter of fact, I was so big the doctor thought I was having twins at first, and for about two months, I ate for three.

At that moment, Rick followed the nurse into the room. She showed us how to adjust the car seat, and we loaded everything up and headed home. I carried the baby into the house. On the table were a bouquet of daisies, a card, and a toy for Jason.

I hugged Rick. "You did think of us." I wanted to cry, but it had nothing to do with postpartum or PMS. Women have tender hearts and just naturally cry over things like that.

CHAPTER 7
Out to Lunch

I'D NEVER GET DRESSED AGAIN. THERE WAS NO POINT—Jason was always out to lunch. When he was out to lunch, "they" were out to lunch. By "they," I mean his lunch conveyors. When "they" were out to lunch, I was out to lunch because, like it or not, we were attached.

I now spent my life in an overstuffed chair that sat in the corner of the room. Thank goodness it wasn't by the window—I couldn't keep my clothes on. I wore my pajama bottoms, and I would have liked to wear a top, but I didn't own enough shirts; my lunch faucets wouldn't turn off. Sometimes the milk came so fast that Jason couldn't even keep up. By the time he was finished, we both needed to be hosed down.

One morning I decided it would save time and energy if I sat in the bathtub all day. When Jason was hungry, he could have at it while I leaked away to my heart's content. If all they said about milk baths was true, I was in for a spa treatment. I filled the tub with hot water, let

Jason sleep in a wicker basket on the floor beside me and climbed in. I leaned back, closed my eyes, and dozed off.

Before long, I realized that there was a reason pillows are not made out of porcelain. I hefted myself up. Water sloshed over the rolls of fat that hid my curves and created a tidal wave. Jason would have drowned, but, just like in the story of Moses, he floated away. The water was frigid, so I pulled myself out. My body had taken on a bluish-purple tinge. I cursed the full-length mirror I'd insisted on hanging. I looked like a kissing cousin to a giant, wrinkled prune.

Back when I'd first decided to breast-feed, I'd had no idea what I was getting into, and women won't tell you. All I remember hearing about was how breast milk was healthy for the baby and about the magic of bonding. There's a lot of propaganda out there, but nothing warned me that nursing would be like running my breasts through a wringer washer.

I don't know how babies are educated about the whole breast-feeding thing before they arrive on earth, but if there is some heavenly class, a lot of them flunked. The valedictorians take to it naturally. They are placid, and they politely sup. The class clowns fuss about, won't latch on right, and tease you with a half-smile as milk drips down their chin. They leave both of you sopping wet and exhausted. Then there's the sucker from—well, you know where. These are the athletic types, the meat eaters. Each time they finish eating, you pull your nails from the arm of the chair and check to be sure you don't need spare parts.

My nurse at the hospital was the only one who gave me any helpful advice. She said to hold a light bulb inches away from the nipple after nursing to toughen it up. I almost scorched myself a couple of times, but it worked.

I would have enjoyed the whole nursing experience a lot sooner if I had found something to hold back the flow of the milky-way. I don't know who invented nursing pads, but it was not a nursing mother. They are as effective as tissue paper in a flood.

I knew I could not live the next year of my life sitting in my chair and stuffing my bra with bath towels. At some point, I would have to venture out, and the world was not ready to see me slogging down the street with soggy bath towels dripping beneath my shirt.

I found the answer hiding under the bathroom sink: Kotex maxi pads. Now there was something with soaking power. Not only that, but they molded perfectly where I needed them to mold. They didn't distort my figure like a bath towel did, and if they added another extra inch to my cup size, I was grateful—it made my stomach look smaller.

It had to happen; one day I ran out.

Men have a universal aversion to buying female products. A Tibetan friend of mine once sent her husband to the store for Kotex. He couldn't find them, so he had to ask the sales girl. He was embarrassed, and that made his accent worse. At last she nodded and took him to look at the Kodak cameras. When she finally did get the message through pantomime, they were both humiliated.

I can't say I blame men for not being eager to make such a purchase—I hate to buy the things myself. It's not so bad if you have other groceries to hide them under. I don't know why they isolate them on their own shelf. They should blend them in with the breakfast cereal or some other colorfully packaged food so you can choose them discreetly. When you're constipated or have hemorrhoids, for instance, it's not so humiliating when someone catches you in that aisle. You could be looking for bandages, headache pills, or other medicinal items.

Personally, I think Kotex should come in the mail wrapped in plain brown paper. But since it doesn't, there was only one thing to do: "Honey, can you help me please? I need a little, bitty favor."

"I am not going to buy your girlie . . . stuff. Last time I was lucky not to get arrested."

I bit down hard on the inside of my lower lip to keep from laughing; I remembered. When he came home and told me what had happened, he had been so embarrassed his ears were still red. It was so funny that I kept waking up in the middle of the night to laugh some more. I can still picture him, walking up and down the aisles, trying to blend in.

He had pulled his hat over his eyes, tugged the collar of his coat up around his ears, and checked to see if anyone was watching. He must have looked like a thug casing the joint. He grabbed the offensive box, scoped out the vicinity again, and then tucked it inside his jacket.

As he skulked to the checkout with his booty, the store detective grabbed his elbow and asked to see the item bulging under his coat. There he stood at the front of the store, a crowd of prying eyes turned in his direction, while he tried to explain why he would never steal a box of sanitary napkins. Lucky for him, the man was married and could commiserate. Rick hadn't set foot in that store since.

"Honey, you have to go to the store. I soak through my entire wardrobe every day, my incision hurts, and I can hardly walk. Not only that, but you do not have the right equipment to take care of Jason." Wow. I had hidden talents. I was able to say all that and still bite my lip.

"Look," said Rick. "I've got some duct tape in the basement. We've got that extra-absorbent toilet paper. How about I duct tape a roll of toilet paper to each side? That ought to hold you."

"Great idea. While you're at it, maybe you could roll up two big poster boards and make a funnel to tape on the end of the toilet paper rolls. That way, you could sit across the room and bond with the baby while he waits for the milk to run from me, through the toilet paper roll, and into the funnel so you can feed him. Are you crazy?"

"Well, look on the bright side. You'd never run out of toilet paper in a public restroom."

If I had rolled my eyes any further into the back of my head they'd have been lost behind my brain.

"All right," he finally agreed, "but this is absolutely the last time. I don't care if you have to crawl in the snow, uphill both ways, with the baby duct taped to your back while he nurses through one of your stupid poster board funnels, I am never buying those . . . things again."

"You're too good to me, honey."

Half an hour later, Rick grunted his way into the living room. I could barely see his eyes behind a huge case emblazoned with bold letters—Kotex Maxi Pads.

"What the heck are you doing? How did you get that thing home and why?"

Rick dropped it onto the floor. "Where do you want these?"

"I want you to take them back where you got them. Do you plan on renting a storage unit? How did you get them here, anyway? With a tow truck?"

"Nope." Rick sat on the corner of the box and grinned. "I tied it to the top of the car."

"You call that being inconspicuous? Did the neighbors see you?"

"Well, I got thinking. It's embarrassing to parade up to the front of the store with a little blue box of pads that my wife could buy for herself, so I decided to make it look like I was there for an emergency, you know, something a man has to do. I marched up to the checker and told her I needed the biggest, baddest box of maxi pads she had in the store. She asked for my name and then got on the intercom: 'We need a dolly up front with a deluxe carton of Super Maxi Pads for Mr. Rick Still, please.'"

I could feel my face turn white and my stomach churn. "Didn't she think it was strange that you needed so many?"

"I just told her, 'Heavy flow. Don't ask.'"

Well, that made two stores we'd never shop in again. If this kept up, we'd be buying our groceries out-of-state. On the upside though, now that I had plenty of the proper equipment, I was ready to venture back into the real world.

CHAPTER 8
Operation Fumigation

MOTHERHOOD HAD CHANGED ME. MOST women became nurturing and unselfish after giving birth. For me, it brought out my criminal tendencies. It all began with diapers.

In my pre-baby days, I was an authority on everything I knew nothing about. I was like an "annoy" button that would just go off for no reason and share my uneducated opinion on any mothering topic that was shaking around loose in my brain. One of those topics was diapers. At any gathering of two or more women, I could be counted on to espouse my views on this highly intellectual issue. On one occasion, I even sat down with a pen and paper to convince Rick, with facts and figures, exactly how and why it was so economical to use cloth. I liked to remind him how lucky he was to be married to someone who was willing to sacrifice convenience for the good of the family.

Looking back, I realize that none of this was my fault. I had been brainwashed. Trisha and Tammy, two of my college roommates, were engaged and spent hours giggling and laughing over finalizing wedding plans and making diapers. Not just any diapers, but cute ones with baby animals, like ducks and rabbits, stamped and then hand painted on the backsides. They constantly extolled the virtues of cloth, the two main arguments being cost and healthy, breathable cotton against the baby's bottom.

I was an enthusiastic wannabe. Sometime in the far-distant future, I wanted everything they would have. So, while they each made one set, I made three. The only thing I had in my hope chest when I got married was thirty-six soft, absorbent baby chick diapers that I'd spent months toiling over.

My fluffy white diapers were folded and stacked, with their painted bottoms up, when I came home from the hospital with Jason. In less than an hour, he had violated one of my masterpieces in a disgusting way. No amount of scrubbing would ever restore it. My roommates were insane.

For the next few days, I cursed my big mouth as I rinsed, washed, and folded diapers. My brain focused on one thing: How to con my husband into begging me to give up cloth for disposables. If he was going to be buying them for our next twelve children, it had to be his idea. Besides, I wasn't about to admit I was wrong. I owed it to our marriage not to jeopardize his confidence in me.

My first plan of attack was to gather reinforcements. I called my sister Celia (who was lucky enough to have had twins) and begged her to use some of my cloth diapers and bring them back to me dirty. Operation Fumigation was set to start when Rick came home for lunch.

"Honey, what's that smell?" Rick sucked in a whiff of air as he walked in the door.

"Your lunch," I said with a smile.

"I'm not eating anything that smells like it climbed out of the sewer."

"Oh, that. Remember I told you how breathable cloth diapers would be? I was right. We're breathing them right now. Refreshing, in a natural sort of way, isn't it?"

"Don't we have any bleach?" Rick asked as he came over to examine his lunch.

"Bleach, umm . . . I think I used the last of it yesterday. We need some more, and while you're picking it up, we need laundry soap and fabric softener too."

"I just bought bleach. What are you doing, drinking it?"

"Not funny, hon," I called after him as he walked out of the room. "By the way, I think Jason is developing a diaper rash from the bleach. My cousin Sharon says we need to buy something to soak our diapers in and rinse them again to get rid of detergent build up. Get some of that stuff too. I can't remember the name of it. Just ask at the store."

"Jane, why is there a diaper in the toilet?"

"Use the other bathroom."

"What am I supposed to do, go outside?" he called. "There's a diaper in this one too."

"Honey, I'm trying to finish making your lunch. Just rinse it out and throw it in the pail. And since you mentioned it, there are some dirty diapers on the back porch that need attention. Do you mind?"

Rick came walking back into the kitchen. "Are you kidding me? You want me to hose them down or something? Isn't there some kind of law against that kind of contamination? I'll stir the soup. You go flush the diapers."

"Honey, it's not that difficult. You're going to have to learn sometime. I'll show you." I turned off the soup and dragged Rick into the bathroom. "Just grab the diaper and swish it, then flush. It's easy."

"Jane, this is not in my scope of practice."

"Ha ha, you're not a doctor yet, and when it comes to the baby anything under my scope of practice—except the physically impossible, of course—will always be under your scope of practice. So get practicing. Here, I'll help. You swirl, and I'll flush."

"What are you doing?" Rick yelled as I flushed, and the toilet sucked up the diaper. "I didn't have a good hold. Grab the plunger."

"You're not supposed to let go," I shrieked as the water spewed out of the toilet. I leaped into the tub. "Make it stop!"

Rick bent behind the toilet and turned the water off while I threw some towels in his general direction.

"Look," I said. "There's a corner of the diaper. Reach in and get it."

Rick turned and glared. "You, Princess Flusher, are going to pull out the diaper and clean up this mess. I'm going to change my pants, eat my soup, and go back to school."

With that, he shut the door and left me in the flooded bathroom. I started to chuckle softly. "Wow, that went better than I expected. Score one for inconvenience. Now to work on the pocketbook."

"Honey, you have to do something about the smell in here," was Rick's greeting when he came home later that day. "The stench is going to start permeating our clothes. People are going to start calling us the Smell family instead of the Still family."

Like I didn't know that? I'd been carrying the diaper pail around from room to room all day for effect. I'd even stashed some dirty diapers under the couch for good measure. I had to dip cotton swabs into perfume and shove them up my nose just to keep my eyes from watering. Life would have been so much easier if I'd been born mute to begin with.

"Hi, hon. Does it really smell that bad? You'll get used to it. How was school? I got the diaper out of the toilet, in case you're interested."

"Do we need a twelve bathroom house now? Or can we manage with two?" Rick asked as he walked around the house opening windows.

"There are no diapers in the toilets, if that's what you're getting at. Did you remember to pick up the laundry soap, the rinse agent, the fabric softener, and the bleach?"

"Janie, are cloth diapers worth all this? My nose is in permanent recoil. It's not built for this kind of assault."

"Well, I guess they do get riper with age. Kind of like fine wine or cheese."

"Cheese, maybe; wine, no. You actually wash these things in water, right? You're not just swishing them around wasting the products?"

"Don't be ridiculous. Jason just gives new meaning to the term, 'little stinker.' Actually, I've been talking to Sharon. She figured out that when you count the extra products and the rise in electricity, not to mention the inconvenience, disposable diapers are a lot cheaper. What do you think?"

"How about we take all these diapers and have a big bonfire with lots of smoke? We can fan it into the house and smoke the stench out."

I nodded my head and smiled. "What a great idea. We could call it Operation Fumigation."

CHAPTER 9
Booby Trapped

JASON AND I WERE ABOUT TO MAKE OUR debut into the controversial world of nursing in public. We were having a family dinner at the in-laws. Everyone in the immediate family would be there: Rick's two brothers, his sister, their corresponding spouses, and the doting grandparents.

Dinner was finished;

Jason had been "ooh"ed and "aah"ed over and had been asleep on Grandma's lap for some time. In the middle of my animated version of the events that had transpired since his birth, he began to fuss. Panic hit. I felt like a hot air balloon being inflated just before lift off. I expected myself to float away at any second. It was feeding time.

During childbirth, all my modesty and decorum had vanished. I would have enthusiastically embraced the chance to lie naked in the streets of New York City while the entire cast and crew of Good Morning America examined me on national television if it would have alleviated my pain. Yet now, in the bosom of this family with whom I had shared tents, drinking glasses, and outdoor bathrooms, I was having a modesty attack.

I closed my eyes for a moment to come up with a nursing technique that would not break any laws of decency. Moments like this confirmed to me that, at the appropriate time, I must gift my brain to science. I could feel my right and left brain stretch inside out and sideways in a race to see which side would be the first to spit out the perfect solution. I don't know which half came up with the Incredible Hulk. It wasn't what I expected, but I was strangely comforted. Here was a member of the opposite sex who knew exactly what I was going through. He knew how it felt to have his body strain beneath his shirt and to realize that it was coming off no matter how inconvenient. It didn't matter if it happened while sitting in church, walking down a busy sidewalk, or eating in a formal restaurant. He too felt the panic of that moment. No wonder he turned green and got angry. I felt a little green too. But if he could get through it, so could I.

I'd seen other mothers discreetly use a blanket in public. How hard could it be? Rick handed the baby to me. Men. They always got the easy job. My insides were jelly, but my hand was steady as I reached into the diaper bag for the thin little receiving blanket. Why hadn't I thought to bring one of the quilts? I placed the skimpy blanket over Jason's head and tucked it behind my shoulder with a move that I hoped looked smooth and nonchalant. I glanced up. All eyes were glued to my chest. Then they all snapped away at the same time. I wanted to bolt, but I couldn't think how to do it gracefully. I reached under the blanket and opened my shirt. Jason knew dinner was about to be served, and I soon discovered there were more ways to be humiliated. He jerked his head back and forth under the blanket and snorted. I fumbled for the fastener on my nursing bra. It twisted and turned between my fingers and refused to come undone. I reached for the other side. Somehow it was twisted in the blanket and would not release. I flashed a gritted smile around the room and discreetly kicked Rick's leg.

"Ow!"

"Oh, I'm sorry."

I turned my smile on him while my eyes bored into his with the unmistakable message: "Help." He didn't get it. I had to see what I was doing, so I attempted to maneuver the blanket off my shoulder and over my head. The flimsy thing may as well have been a postage stamp for all the modesty it afforded. Fortunately, Jason had found his fist and was appeased for the moment. I pulled my head back out and kicked Rick again.

"Ow."

"Oh, did you hurt yourself, dear?"

I smiled at the room, then turned glacial eyeballs on Rick and hissed, "Get me a bigger blanket." Jason was snorting and rubbing his head conspicuously back and forth under the blanket again, and the blanket started to slide. I reached down and grabbed a corner with my teeth. I batted my eyes at the room and continued to smile, as though a mouthful of cloth were the most natural thing in the world.

Rick finally arrived with a quilt. He hurled it on top of me and knocked over the lamp that sat on a table next to us. It crashed to the floor, and Jason started crying. The quilt weighed at least a hundred pounds and was big enough to shelter a herd of elephants. What was the man thinking?

I hefted the blanket over my head. I couldn't see a thing, and I started to sweat. Jason was screaming now, and his head was wet. I tried to fight my way out of the sweatbox with one hand and hold onto Jason with the other. Were these people blind? We were about to suffocate in front of the whole family, and they were sitting there exchanging pleasantries.

I caught a glimpse of daylight and reached in that direction. I popped my head out, pulled Jason into the fresh air, and passed him to his daddy. I reached back under the quilt to adjust the receiving blanket around me and preserve a little dignity. Everyone looked a little startled when I leaped to my feet and announced, "The baby needs changing." I grabbed the diaper bag and rushed upstairs.

Oh crap! I had forgotten the baby. Now what? I turned around. "Thank you," I whispered and looked toward heaven. Rick had followed me out with Jason.

"Why did you kick me?"

"Honey, first of all, when I kick you, don't ever say, 'Ow.'"

"Well, then don't kick so hard." He passed Jason to me.

"What are you, the princess and the pea or something? Your shins aren't that delicate. When I kick you, it's for a reason. I needed help. I was trying to feed your son, and that contraption I'm wearing would not come undone."

"Why didn't you just tell me? What am I, a mind reader?"

"Yeah, like I'm going to announce to your entire family that I'm an imbecile and can't even feed my baby without help? I was telling you with my eyes."

"Janie, I don't read eyes."

"Stop laughing. It's not funny. What did you want me to do, throw it all out there and invite everyone to watch the picnic?"

"Well, at least I wouldn't be limping now."

Jason started to fuss. This poor child had waited long enough. I kicked Rick again. "Public communication lesson number one: When I kick you and do this," I squinted my eyes and tried to look mad, "it means 'I . . . need . . . help.'"

I escaped into the closest bedroom and locked the door. I lay down with Jason while he ate and listened to Rick hopping around on one foot. He was laughing so hard I thought he'd fall over.

"I hope you fall and bang your head," I shouted. He roared even louder.

What the heck was Rick laughing about? I was wearing a nursing bra designed by Houdini, he—my husband—had practically snuffed out my life with the quilt of death, and I had forgotten to bring a spare shirt. Why couldn't we have do-overs? Days we could wipe out and do again?

CHAPTER 10
The Diaper Bag

ON THEIR OWN, A FEW
DIAPERS, BOTTLES, cans
of formula, sippy cups, a change
of baby clothes, Kotex for nursing,
receiving blankets, quilts, wet wipes,
ointment, lotion, soothers, toys, all the
essentials from my purse, a camera, and
a water bottle don't weigh much. But
all together, cramming stuff into my
diaper bag was like packing for a
mini vacation every time I left
home. Most airlines would have
made me pay a surcharge.

It was always a grim moment
when I traded my purse in for
that little accessory just smaller than
a steamer trunk. No matter how elegant

I tried to look, I felt like a pack mule when I slung on my diaper bag. It cut such deep grooves into my shoulders that my children were teenagers before I discovered the grooves weren't permanent after all.

I could never figure out how other women managed to keep their bags looking so pristine. In a matter of weeks, mine were always christened with sour milk from leaky bottles that streaked down the sides and permeated the air like the scent from a cheese factory. Every time I pulled out a necessity, crushed Cheerios and crackers would fly into the air like a swarm of mosquitoes. My bag always looked like I had left it in a barn with wild goats that had stomped, chewed, and spit on it. It was so disgusting, I had to buy a new one for every baby.

Selecting the right bag from the overstocked shelves in the department store brought out all of my insecurities. It forced me to sort through my multiple personalities and pick one that would be my signature statement for the next year and a half of my life.

With Jason, I didn't realize a diaper bag was such a status symbol, and the one the hospital gave me with the orange hippo appliquéd on the side just seemed to resonate with how I looked and felt.

By the time Ariana was born, I was sensitive to the message it advertised to the world. Orange hippo shouted "novice" not "dignified." So, when I was pregnant with Ariana, I began to pay attention to the type of bags women were sporting in the baby kingdom.

The conservative bargain-hunting moms wore a denim jumper, Mary Poppins shoes, and a ho-hum hairdo. They carried a quilted, washable bag lined in red bandana fabric that definitely did not sing my song. I was more of a high heels and wild hair kind of mom.

My sister was one of those organized women who carried a cloth bag lined with plastic that she considered to be on the cutting edge. It had little compartments for every item imaginable, and it unfolded into a changing mat. She had the opportunity to organize herself into insanity because every time she wanted to change her baby, it had to be unpacked before she could lay her little darling on it.

It reminded me of the coat worn by thugs in a movie. You know, the guy who stands on the street corner and furtively opens his coat to display watches and other ill-gotten booty he wants to pawn off onto some unsuspecting patsy. My sister's bag was only on the market for a few months—big surprise. I was looking for flash and sophistication, not aggravation.

I found flash and sophistication in the Cadillac of all bags with a price tag to match. Fifty dollars was a huge chunk out of our tiny budget in the early eighties, especially for an item that wasn't made of tooled leather and lined in gold. But the longer I gazed at it, the more I lusted for the smooth black bag with shiny silver snaps on the side pockets. It looked sharp and sophisticated in a non-hippo sort of way.

The criminal element in my mind began to sneak out as I schemed about how to pay for it. I couldn't exactly say I'd won the lottery.

I used to get money for things like this while I went through my Dad's pockets on laundry day. But Rick's pockets just yielded boring notes he took in school.

My one hope was to get creative with the only resource I had: the grocery budget. With a little imagination, I could make beans the new vogue. Refried bean soufflé, ground black bean bread, and even pinto bean fudge. Rick would never notice as long as I slapped on lots of ketchup and mixed it with hot sauce. Besides, beans were much healthier. Didn't it say somewhere in my marriage vows that I was obligated to love and cherish him " 'til death do us part?" I would be saving him from death-by-hamburger.

I'd give my sister the money and have her buy it for me. If I hid it in my closet for a while, I could honestly say that Celia bought it for me ages ago. After all, wouldn't it help Rick's future career if I learned to dress for success? What kind of wife would I be if I tried to sabotage him with gross fashion faux pas like sporting an orange hippo on my hip?

I hoped Rick would appreciate how exhausting it was for me to constantly think of ways to sacrifice for his success and for the family. He would never know of my selflessness. I definitely deserved this bag.

When all was said and done, I have to admit there was one perk to lugging around my little steamer trunk. I could stash all my emergency supplies: milk chocolate, dark chocolate, white chocolate, caramel chocolate, mint chocolate, square chocolate, round chocolate, striped chocolate, chocolate kisses, chocolate-covered raisins, chocolate-covered nuts and—for my sweet tooth—some red hots to satisfy any craving at a moment's notice.

My children, husband, and other innocent bystanders were saved from many unpleasant moments by my chocolate induced trances. When the children started screaming in decibels that defied every law of nature, and when pulling each hair out of my nose with tweezers started to sound like a relaxing day at the spa, I simply grabbed my candy factory and squeezed us both into the nearest dark closet. It was like being cocooned in a little slice of heaven.

I was finally forced to give up the closet. Not because of any emotional maturity on my part, but because Rick came home early unexpectedly one day and caught me in my sanctuary. There I was, squinting up at the bright light and making slobbery noises, my cheeks puffed out like a giant squirrel with a ten years' supply of nuts stashed away in my mouth. I am probably the only woman in history who has been grounded from her diaper bag.

CHAPTER 11
Getting Back into the Swing of Things

ANY FEMININE MYSTIQUE I LIKED TO THINK I once exuded had melted away, and I was too tired to care. It had been months since I had even felt like using my feminine wiles. There wasn't much time for a lot of alluring to be done, either. I wondered if I'd ever feel like being alluring again.

My whole aura had changed. I quit wearing dangly earrings when Jason jerked on a hoop and almost tore off my lobe. Falling off three-inch, spiked heels felt like stepping off a skyscraper when I was carrying a baby, so I was back to wearing my squat, ugly shoes. Jason's chubby little fist was like an iron claw he liked to twist in my hair and yank. When it got to the point that I was checking my scalp for blood, I had my hair cut. After that, I woke up with bed hair every morning. It was depressing.

But tonight I was ready to don the hoops and heels. Rick was taking me out on our first official date since Jason had been born. It was time to pull back the cobwebs and shake the dust from my wardrobe. There must be something in there I could cram myself into by now.

The maternity clothes had to go. I pulled them off the hangers, boxed, them up, and shoved them under the bed. My closet was considerably thinner now. I was jealous. My T-shirts, a reminder of my wily days, beckoned me from the top shelf. I pulled them down, hugged them to my chest, and breathed in the essence of the girl I used to be—the one with the flat chest and trim waistline. I piled them in a bottom drawer that I mentally tagged, "Someday Soon."

I rummaged through a pile of jeans crammed in a dark corner. Did I dare? I pulled out a favorite pair. "Careful now, don't get too excited." I was speaking to the girl in the mirror. "They're sliding up, over the thighs, past the hips." One more major obstacle and . . . "Yes!" I screamed. They had encompassed the tush and pulled around the front. Four more inches, and I'd have a home run.

I took a deep breath to suck my stomach in. It wouldn't suck. I tried to flatten it with my hands and stuff it somewhere, anywhere. It wasn't happening. I tugged at the zipper. Nothing. If I could just snap them shut, I could cover the zipper with a shirt. I tugged and then pulled again, harder. I backed against the wall, spread my feet apart, braced myself, and tried again. It was close. I felt light headed from all the huffing and puffing, so I rested on the edge of the bed.

This must be how girls felt years ago when they had to wear whalebone corsets to achieve those ridiculous waistlines that could be spanned by a man's hands. No wonder they had to have someone hold a foot in their back and pull at the strings. That's it! I jumped up. "Rick, I need help. And bring the pliers."

"You want me to what?"

"I want you to snap up my pants."

"Honey, you're regressing. Do we have two babies in the house now? Should I be worried about potty training time?"

I punched him. "Did you think that up all by yourself? If I can button your long-sleeved shirts for you, you can snap my pants up for me."

"Turn around then." He reached from behind and pulled and tugged my waistband forward.

"Ow. You're pinching me." I pushed his hands away and turned to face him.

"Jane, this is humanly impossible. It can't be done. When a snake outgrows its skin, it gets a bigger one."

"Thanks a lot. In case you didn't notice, I am not a snake, and I don't want bigger jeans. I want smaller ones."

"Is that supposed to make sense?"

"You don't understand. Let's try this. You pull the top as close together as you can, and I'll try to get the zipper closed."

Rick stood in front of me, grabbed each side, and pulled.

"Not so hard. You're knocking me over. Let's go over there so I can brace against the wall."

"Honey—"

"Don't say it; you're only here for your brute strength. Now pull." I braced myself, held my breath, and tugged on the zipper while he tried to force the snap shut. The zipper kept slipping out of my fingers. "I need those pliers."

"I'm telling you, hon, this defies every known law of physics. No two objects can occupy the same space at the same time."

"I hate it when you tell me something can't be done. Remember when your mom wanted the washer moved into her new house? You, your dad, and every male cousin within a sixty-mile radius—plus all the neighbors up the street—tried to move it into her laundry room. Every single one of you threw up your hands and said it was impossible. Well, didn't mom and I finally do it? By ourselves, I might add. Women know how to fit big things into small spaces. It comes naturally."

Rick looked over at the open drawer that held my T-shirts. "You can say that again. All right, I'll try one more time, but just remember you're not a worm. If these pants cut you in two . . . ." He pulled his thumb across his neck.

I slapped my arms against the wall, braced, and took a deep breath. "Pull." They snapped. "See? That was easy."

Rick started to laugh. "Uh, honey, what are you going to do with that?" He pointed at the rolls of fat pouring out where the zipper wouldn't close.

"Gimme the pliers."

"I think a butcher knife would be a better choice," he said.

"Ha ha. I'm not the only one that could stand a little artful carving. At least I have an excuse."

I turned back to the closet and threw some shirts on the bed that might reach over the gaping hole. They were all too short and didn't have a prayer of buttoning. I had another idea and grabbed a jacket. "Pass me one of my T-shirts." Rick raised his eyebrows.

I stretched the shirt over my head, pushed my arms into the sleeves, and pulled. So far so good. Mount Everest had been conquered—just barely. But, hopefully, it would be enough. I slipped my arms into the jacket and fastened the button at the waistline. It was snug, and the button pulled, but hey, it was on. I looked in the mirror.

My pants still bulged open below my jacket, and my T-shirt missed covering my stomach by a whole two inches. Not to mention that it looked like someone had attacked me with fuchsia colored paint. My shirt was so stretched out that if I'd had a mole you'd know it.

I caught sight of Rick lying on the floor with his hands over his mouth and his legs kicking the air. He gasped a breath between snorts and tried to hold in the laughter. When we made eye contact, he let it all go.

"Honey, don't do this to me. I can't stand it," he gasped, wiping his eyes from his fit of hysterics. "This is better than *Freebie and the Bean*." He started howling again.

"Okay, mister, forget the movies. We're going shopping."

He couldn't stop holding his stomach and rolling around the floor. I felt a smile tug the corners of my mouth, but he wasn't going to see it. I crossed my arms, grabbed the bottom of my shirt, and yanked.

My arms were trapped, and my T-shirt wouldn't budge over my head. I tugged harder. I knew Rick saw my predicament because he was hiccupping for breath now. He tried to speak but couldn't. I wanted to go stomp on him, but I couldn't see where he was.

"Would you get off the floor and help me? My arms are breaking, and I can't breathe." I heard him crawl into the bathroom.

"What are you doing? I am about to die a humiliating death-by-T-shirt, with all this flab hanging out of my pants for the entire world to see plastered over their TV screens, and you choose this precise moment to go to the bathroom? I can see the headlines now: 'Man Chooses Call of Nature over Wife Screaming.' Is that what you want? To put another nail in the family values coffin?"

As he came back into the room, I could hear the high-pitched voice he got when he laughed so hard he couldn't speak. "Stop, stop—," there was a pause while he tried to suck in some air, "—or I will die." I heard him fall back onto the bed.

"Either you help me right now, or I'm going to stand in the street and shout for 911."

"Stop," he pleaded. I could feel his body heaving as he stood up beside me. There was no strength in his arms as he tried to pull my shirt off. We collapsed together backwards onto the bed.

Now I really was going to die. Not only was I smothering, but I couldn't breathe for laughing either. At last Rick got enough control to pull my shirt free. My face was wet with tears and sweat. I put my hands on my stomach to calm down. My stomach was gone. I reached for my zipper. It zipped.

"Look, it's a miracle. I did my pants up. Stop laughing. You've run your quota for the day." I grabbed his hand. "Feel. It's flat. What happened?" The law of gravity had saved me.

Rick wiped his eyes and took a last couple of chuckles. "So, what shirt are you going to wear?"

"Get me one of your T-shirts."

He rummaged through the closet and threw a shirt at me. I tried to get up. "I can't move; it's like I'm wearing a back brace or something. Give me your hand."

He reached out and pulled me up. I couldn't bend. "You're not going to be able to walk in those pants, let alone sit. We'll have to rent a dolly. I pulled his T-shirt over my head and tied it in a knot at my waist.

"I can walk just fine." I staggered stiffly to the mirror and turned sideways. "Look how thin I am. Get me another mirror—I want to see the back." Rick grabbed my hand mirror, and I held it up.

"Do they look too tight?"

"Wait, I'll grab some turpentine to rub off the paint, and then I'll airbrush on a bigger pair," he said.

"Maybe I could light a match to your moustache and watch your nose hairs burn. Throw me my coat. I'm doing this." Rick reached into the closet for my coat.

"You'd better put your hat on. You'll be cold up there tied down to the roof of the car," he said.

"Why don't you start supporting our family by being a stand-up comedian if you think you're so funny? Then I can lose weight the old fashioned way: starvation."

I stuck my chin in the air and did the Frankenstein clomp to the kitchen table. "I'll prove I can sit." I pulled out a chair. My right arm gripped the edge of the table, and I tried to lower myself into a sitting position. Okay, I could get creative. I pushed the chair back until I could balance myself on the end. "There. If you push the car seat all the way back, I can prop myself up on it like this."

"It'll be like driving with a teeter-totter," said Rick.

"I feel so cherished."

"Ah, honey." He reached down and threw me over his shoulder like a board. "Allow me to load you into the front seat."

I didn't care what the neighbors or anyone else said. My jeans had zipped, and my husband could still lift me. I began to feel alluring again.

CHAPTER 12
What Did I Say about Children?

"HONEY, DO YOU THINK IT'S TOO EARLY to start spanking Jason?" I clapped my hands over my mouth and whined through my fingers. "I want my money back from that stupid child development class. If I had that guy's phone number, I'd tell him a thing or two." In my wildest dreams, I could never have imagined the questions I should have asked in that class to prepare me for what I desperately needed to know.

"You're just suffering from sleep deprivation, hon. My mom says it passes in about twenty years."

I threw my current book, *Raising the Perfect Child*, across the room. "Jason keeps tearing all the books out of the bookcase, and nothing I do seems to faze him."

Rick picked the book off the floor and thumbed through the pages. "It says right here that all you have to do is be consistent."

"Well, guess what. Your son is a dud. He doesn't know how to read."

"Obviously, you're just not being consistent enough."

"Well, I say I am!" I exploded. "It's not like I have a lot of anything else to do. You don't have to be a brain surgeon to know if you're being consistent or not. Do you think we should spank him? You know, just a little swat on the bottom. Is he old enough?"

We'd been having this discussion for several days. I'd been beginning to suspect for a while now that maybe there was a little more to this child raising business than I had originally thought. It wasn't as though I could ask one of my friends. I was the resident pro who had spent the last year telling everyone else how to raise their children. I considered pulling a paper bag over my head so no one would recognize me when I went out in public these days.

"We just have to be consistent," Rick reiterated.

"You want to see consistency? This child knows consistency."

I lifted Jason out of his swing and set him on the floor. It wasn't one minute before he had crawled to the bookcase and pulled the books onto the floor. We took turns pulling him away. Even Mr. "All-you-have-to-do-is-be-consistent" began to consistently give him a gentle swat on the bottom each time. Jason in turn would consistently cry and head right back to the bookcase. After an hour or two of entertaining ourselves in this manner, we wore ourselves out and put Jason to bed.

In the middle of the night, I had a brainstorm. I jumped out of bed, took all the books off the bottom shelf and put his toys there instead.

The next morning, true to form, Jason headed straight for the bookcase. This time, however, he left the books alone and played with his toys.

"Ha," I gloated. "I guess I outsmarted you."

At that very moment, as he looked into my eyes and smiled, the awful truth washed over me. My child was smarter than I was, and I would lose many more battles before it was all over.

"Oh, well," I said, sighing. "At least when he's a teenager, I'll be able to reason with him.

CHAPTER 13
You Oughta Be in Pictures

ONE DAY I GATHERED MY SIX CHILDREN together and announced that we were going to make their scrapbooks. We sorted through all of their crates. Jason had to take his fifteen into a different part of the house, so he could spread out. Briana, my youngest, sorted her little envelope out on the end table and didn't even have to move the lamp. She looked at me with her big brown eyes and asked, "Didn't you love me, Mom?"

If she had driven a dull knife in my heart and twisted, it couldn't have hurt more.

Once the initial shock of seeing Jason for the first time had worn off, I was stunned by that fact that my loins had produced the most beautiful creation on the planet. I wanted to cuddle him every second. When his grandma (the unfeeling woman) or anyone else was insensitive enough to rip him from my arms, I had to stifle the urge to put a stake through their heart.

I should have gone with my first instincts. It was many years before I was able to look at his baby pictures and see that his eyes were the size of pie plates and that he had been cursed with my weak chin. I realized then that not only is a mother's love blind, but it is also deaf to the creative ways people have of telling you that your baby is freakish.

I was oblivious to the fact that when my cousins called him mouse legs it was not out of endearment. Neither was my sister-in-law being complimentary when she told me that he looked like an X-ray and that every time she bathed him she had to hold onto his ankles to keep him from being sucked down the drain.

He also liked to scratch his bald head. It always had red claw marks on it when I forgot to put his mittens on him. It wouldn't surprise me if, underneath all of his hair, he still bears the tiny fingernail indentations from his early childhood.

He must have inherited his looks from me because the first thing my dad said when he saw me was, "She's ugly. Send her back." But I saw only perfection in Jason and interpreted every statement about him as a compliment that reinforced my opinion of his exquisite characteristics. Didn't we have an obligation to capture every nuance of his personality and beauty on camera? We owed it to the world.

Even though we were poor college students, food was not as important as buying film so we could feast on pictures of our son. We captured every flick of the eyelid and wrinkle of the nose. Our walls were papered with photographs. My mother-in-law commented several times that she had never seen so many family pictures in so little an area.

But Briana was right. As each child came along, we took fewer and fewer pictures until hers were almost nonexistent.

I could fix that. I curled her hair. We selected her cutest outfit and went on a picture-taking binge. She snuffed rose petals into her nose in the garden. She read a book on the library steps, played in a swing with my friend's cat, and sat on the limb of a tree with her doll.

After lunch we had a tea party on the steps with her sisters and fed the ducks at the lake. I laughed when a goose chased her, but then it bit her. I thought she could run faster than that. Then she started to cry, so picture-taking day was over.

Later that evening, I thumbed through Briana's little envelope of pictures and noticed she only had one professional 8 ½ × 11 inch baby picture. It was too late to fix that. Or was it? Kristjana and Briana had looked a lot alike when they were about eighteen months old. Kristjana had several pictures. So I did the only rational thing: I crossed her name out and wrote Briana's in. Who would ever know?

When Jason moved away from home, he had to rent a moving van just for his baby pictures. Briana left with a small box full of pictures from a single day in her life. And she is much cuter than Jason. I was a failure as a mother.

CHAPTER 14

Reverence

I EXAMINED MY WRINKLES ONE FINAL TIME in the mirror. This was what I had to show for all my years as reverence police.

"Honey, do you suppose people at church appreciate how much I've sacrificed the contours of my face in behalf of reverence all these years?"

Rick snorted out a cross between a chuckle and a guffaw and herded the kids into the car to head for our church services.

Not long after, we were seated in our bench. "Do we have 'stupid' written on our foreheads?" I whispered to Rick across the pew. He gave me a curious look. I nodded my head toward the end of the bench. "We must have 'stupid' tattooed all over our foreheads. Why else would parents send their children to sit with us so they can enjoy the meeting?"

For reasons of self-esteem, I decided that those parents had come to recognize my experience and ability in keeping our children reverent and were hoping I could do something with theirs.

Rick, however, was not a friend of reverence. He was an entertainer. How was I to know that that was a critical attribute I should have checked on my long list of "Future Husband Material" requirements?

We used to sit near the back of the chapel before I realized the obvious. My children would never conquer reverence by watching the examples of irreverent children sitting in the benches in front of them. I moved us to the second row, but that failed to solve the problem of my husband.

At church, this quiet, composed man suddenly became a comedian, and he was impervious to the disciplining looks I developed for the children. Rick loved to sneak candy and Cheerios into the chapel. He would stick a Cheerio halfway into his mouth and tease our children to bite the other end. Just as they were about to grab hold, he would jerk his head to one side. When they began to howl, he tickled them until they screamed with laughter. When they finally grasped the candy or Cheerio with their lips, he pretended to be a vacuum cleaner and sucked it back into his mouth. I shudder to imagine what people must have thought of this germ warfare.

"Shh! How can I expect the kids to be quiet if you set this kind of example?"

He was repentant for a moment or two and then exchanged Eskimo and butterfly kisses with the children. With utter disregard to the hours I spent fixing their hair and dressing them, he briskly whisker-rubbed them and threw them into the air.

When it was time to sing, he created hurricane-force winds by whipping their arms in triple time to the chorister's beat.

It probably wasn't his fault. My mother-in-law liked to entertain the kids in church by pushing her false teeth out while they tried to grab them. Once, Jason managed to pull them out of her mouth. He jumped up and down on the bench and waved them around like a prize trophy. All I could do was smile weakly and nod my head.

People never failed to come and speak to me after church meetings. "You are such a lucky woman. Your husband is so good with your children. We love to watch the fun he has playing with them."

I clenched my teeth and smiled. Great, he got rave reviews. I got wrinkles.

CHAPTER 15
Keep the Guilt and Pass the Chocolate

COULD WE CANCEL MOTHER'S DAY, PLEASE, or rename it? Smother-Your-Mom-in-Chocolate Day would work. That would be the sort of holiday moms would actually look forward to celebrating. There would be no expectations, no indigestion, and no guilt. Except maybe for eating too much chocolate, but we can live with that.

It's not that moms don't like a healthy dose of guilt on a daily basis; it's just that we prefer to be the guilt inflictors not the guilty ones.

Mother's Day is a wonderful concept. Many ideas of how to celebrate that day have nice potential, in theory, like breakfast in bed. Maybe it's just me, but being held hostage in my bed and forced to ignore the crashing and banging of six excited children and their culinarily illiterate father thrashing through my cupboards doesn't smack of festivity.

It's not that I'm unwilling to make sacrifices for my family. After all, I suffered through thirty-six hours of hard labor and countless stitches for each cherub that was now inflicting damage on my kitchen in my honor. But isn't there a statute of limitations on the pain and suffering women must endure?

I thrashed about in my bed, trying not to conjure up pictures of Mother's Days past, but some things make an indelible impression: pancakes stuck to the ceiling, jam inside the toaster—and I didn't even want to know how the electric frying pan made it into the toilet. I had it down to a science exactly how many hours, minutes, and seconds it would take to clean up after Mother's Day. What was amazing to me was that Rick didn't seem to remember that Father's Day was only weeks away, and what comes around goes around.

I smashed a pillow to each ear in an effort to block out the arguing, shushing, and breaking glass. Did they think I was dead? My eyes closed while images of purgatory filled my mind. Finally, giggles and muffled footsteps stopped outside the door, and I heard the big, "Surprise!"

This was my Oscar moment. I dropped my jaw and let my eyes pop out like my children's favorite cartoon characters while I scrutinized the blackened toast, cold greasy bacon, rubbery eggs, and two gigantic glasses of orange juice. I wondered how much time I would spend in the bathroom afterwards.

There was no opportunity to ditch a speck of food into the toilet. Six pairs of eyes feasted on me and regaled every gory detail of my meal.

"Mom, Garret was picking his nose, so Adam rammed his finger up so far inside Garret's nostril it started to bleed. But don't worry; we didn't let any blood get on your eggs."

"Sorry you don't have any milk. Kristjana spilled the whole gallon. But it all went under the refrigerator, so no one will even know."

"Jason broke your best pitcher, Mom."

I put on my best grimace and hoped it passed for a smile as I complimented their efforts. Smiles radiated so brightly, I hardly noticed that my food tasted like charcoal ashes. No actress got paid this well.

After breakfast, my stomach and I sloshed around the house, combing hair and washing faces in a fight against time. Six immaculate children rushed out the door for church while I dragged behind looking like ten miles of bad road.

The service extolled every virtue of motherhood, including some virtues I had never heard of before. Apparently there were mothers who didn't save the biggest piece of pie for themselves and then disguise the fact by covering it with ice cream. Was it really possible some mom out there actually enjoyed breakfast in bed? She was probably married to the Galloping Gourmet.

I wrung out my only Kleenex for the third time. Guilt for my feelings at breakfast sat in the pit of my stomach and floated in an ocean of orange juice. I sniffled, dried my eyes, and resolved to be a better mom.

That was when inspiration hit. I would take control of Mother's Day in our house from then on.

My first plan of attack was to begin campaigning. I would educate my children on how blessed they were to have me for a mom so they could put me up there on a pedestal with the moms that were raved about from the pulpit. I would find opportune moments all year long to remind my children how wonderful I was.

"You know, Briana, you're so lucky to have me for a mom. Not many mothers would pull lice from your head three times in a row. They would shave you bald.

"Ariana, you should be grateful I'm your mom. Most mothers wouldn't take the time to pick up all your clothes from the floor and throw them on the front lawn. They would throw a match in your room and burn them all."

I decided to avoid future breakfasts in bed on Mother's Day by reminding my family that I liked to get up at five. My husband and teenagers hated to get up before ten; they'd love me even more for letting them sleep in. The most important part of my plan was to prepare dinner ahead so my family wouldn't destroy my kitchen.

From then on, I'd spend the day before shopping for and preparing an extraordinary dinner that would require the least amount of work and mess—my family wouldn't be happy throwing just anything together for their loving mother. Shish kebabs would work well. That meal gave the illusion of actually having done work. My family would have to put the food—that would just happen to be chopped and in separate bowls—on the sticks, after all.

I'd plan a simple dessert, keeping in mind that it also must appear special. Strawberry shortcake would be perfect. They couldn't possibly ruin a store-bought cake, strawberries, and a spray of whipping cream.

Now, when my husband and children ask me, half an hour past dinnertime, what glorious feast they can prepare, I ponder a moment, suggest shish kebabs, and then take a well-earned rest.

Oh, and while I am shopping, I will purchase the perfect card. I can be sure at least one of my children will have spent the last of her money on an expensive birthday gift for a friend. It would ruin her Mother's Day not to have a little something for me.

After spending hours on what should take minutes, my family will call me to the feast prepared in my honor. It will be a happy Mother's Day!

Now, if you are all smug and think your Mother's Days are perfect, your husband dotes on you, and your children spoil you, you'd better start digging. Someone is hiding something.

When you find out what it is, just remember—these are the best days of your life. When your little catastrophes have moved on, you'll give anything for traces of blackened toast crumbs in the folds of your blankets.

Enjoy your Mother's Daze!

About the Author

WHEN JANE RETURNED TO CANADA, she met and married Rick Still, who she believes has the distinction of being the only man in history brave enough to give the woman he loves earwax candles for her birthday. They moved around Southern Alberta then had their first baby. They moved back to Cardston, then to Davenport, Iowa, had a baby, moved to Lethbridge, Alberta, had another baby, moved to Newfoundland, had a baby, moved back to Lethbridge, and had two more—six kids in eight years. Jane's sister told her she made it look easy.

They got their U.S. papers and moved to Southern California for a couple of years, then moved to Washington where Jane's husband set up practice as a chiropractor.

One of her philosophies in life is, "Try anything once. If you fail, it's always good for a laugh."

To read more about Jane and her projects, visit **janeisfeldstill.blogspot.com**.

0   26575 53870   0